Fixing Food Waste

Nicolas Brasch

Fixing Food Waste

Text: Nicolas Brasch
Publishers: Tania Mazzeo and Eliza Webb
Series consultant: Amanda Sutera
  Hands on Heads Consulting
Editor: Holly Proctor
Project editors: Annabel Smith and Jarrah Moore
Designer: Leigh Ashforth
Project designer: Danielle Maccarone
Permissions researcher: Helen Mammides
Production controller: Renee Tome

Acknowledgements
We would like to thank the following for permission to reproduce copyright material:

Front cover, p. 10 (bottom): Shutterstock.com/Joaquin Corbalan P; pp. 1 (top), 15: Shutterstock.com/Alexey Borodin; pp. 1 (bottom), 15: iStock.com/tBoyan; p. 4: iStock.com/Chinnapong; p. 5 (top). Getty Images/Westend61, (bottom): Shutterstock.com/Pormezz; p. 6 (top): Alamy Stock Photo/Design Pics Inc, (middle): iStock.com/sultancicekgil, (bottom): iStock.com/Hispanolistic; p. 7 (top): Shutterstock.com/Daisy Daisy, (bottom): iStock.com/vgajic; p. 8: Alamy Stock Photo/Guido Paradisi; p. 9 (top): iStock.com/Baloncici, (bottom): Shutterstock.com/Max Zafiro; p. 10 (top): Alamy Stock Photo/Chris Edgcombe; p. 11: Diego Vaisberg © Cengage Learning Australia Pty Limited; p. 12: iStock.com/Eloi_Omella; p. 13 (middle): iStock.com/Mariia Vitkovska, (top left): Shutterstock.com/jirabu, (top right): iStock.com/cizlawet, (bottom left): Shutterstock.com/Lifestyle Travel Photo, (bottom right): Shutterstock.com/snorkulencija; p. 14: Getty Images/Marccophoto; p. 15 (middle): Getty Images/Bloomberg, (bottom): Alamy Stock Photo/Sergio Azenha; p. 16: iStock.com/Hispanolistic; p. 17: iStock.com/zeljkosantrac; p. 18: Shutterstock.com/Rawpixel.com; p. 19 (top): iStock.com/Engin Ozber, (middle): Alamy Stock Photo/martin berry, (bottom): Alamy Stock Photo/Stephen Frost; p. 20 (top): iStock.com/SDI Productions, (bottom): Shutterstock.com/BearFotos; p. 21 (top): iStock.com/Katharina13, (bottom): Alamy Stock Photo/dpa picture alliance; p. 22 (top): Newspix/John Feder, (bottom): OzHarvest; p. 23: OzHarvest; p. 24 (top): Goterra, (bottom): iStock.com/Alan Owen; p. 25: Goterra; pp. 27–29: Lindsay Edwards Photography © Cengage Learning Australia Pty Limited; p. 30: iStock.com/Image Source.

Every effort has been made to trace and acknowledge copyright. However, if any infringement has occurred, the publishers tender their apologies and invite the copyright holders to contact them.

NovaStar

Text © 2024 Cengage Learning Australia Pty Limited
Illustrations © 2024 Cengage Learning Australia Pty Limited

ISBN 978 0 17 033440 2

Cengage Learning Australia
Level 5, 80 Dorcas Street
Southbank VIC 3006 Australia
Phone: 1300 790 853
Email: aust.nelsonprimary@cengage.com

For learning solutions, visit **cengage.com.au**

Printed in China by 1010 Printing International Ltd
1 2 3 4 5 6 7 28 27 26 25 24

Nelson acknowledges the Traditional Owners and Custodians of the lands of all First Nations Peoples. We pay respect to Elders past and present, and extend that respect to all First Nations Peoples today.

Contents

Food Loss and Food Waste

Throwing Away Food

Do you ever leave uneaten food on your plate after dinner, or some of your lunch in your lunch box?

If so, you probably don't think too much about it. You probably do it because you're not hungry, or you don't like what you've been given.

We all leave uneaten food on our plates sometimes.

Food is thrown away on farms, in homes and in restaurants.

When food is thrown away, it's known either as "food loss" or "food waste". Both are big problems facing the world today.

This book looks at what causes food loss and food waste, and what you and others can do about them.

When food is thrown away it is wasted.

What's the Difference?

Food loss and food waste both involve discarding, or throwing away, food – but there's a difference between them.

Some food loss happens while blueberries are being transported from the farm.

Food loss happens when food is thrown away *before* it gets to you or the place you buy it from. By the time it gets to a shop or your fridge or pantry, the food has probably travelled a long way.

First, food is grown or raised on a farm, or produced in a factory. Then, it is transported to a storage area, where it may have been kept for some time. Finally, the food arrives at a shop, supermarket or restaurant for you to buy. If food is thrown away at any stage along this journey, that's called food loss.

Some food loss happens while blueberries are being stored.

Some food loss happens while blueberries are moved from the storage area to a supermarket.

Food waste happens when food is thrown away *after* it has been delivered to a shop, supermarket or restaurant, or has been bought by a customer.

People waste food during cooking, when food is left over from meals, and when food is left too long in the fridge or the cupboard.

When we throw food away after we've bought it, it's called "food waste".

It's important not to buy more food than we will use.

Problems of Food Loss and Food Waste

A Waste of Resources

You might throw a half-eaten apple into a **compost** bin or compost heap and think, "That's okay, it will just decompose (or break down) in the ground and help the soil to grow more food." Discarded food is good for the soil, so it's much better to put food in a compost bin than in **landfill**. But food waste does far more harm to the environment than good.

Putting food in a compost bin is better than letting it go to landfill, but it is still food waste.

Many **resources** are used to make food. One of them is water, which is **scarce** in a lot of places around the world. Water is needed to grow fruit and vegetable crops, and to raise animals on farms. If food is thrown away after it has been produced, all the water that was used to make that food has been wasted.

A large sprinkler provides water to grow lettuce on a farm.

You've probably been told to use as little water as possible when you have a shower. Well, throwing away a burger is like leaving the shower running for 90 minutes. That shower uses up the same amount of water that's needed to make the ingredients in just one burger!

TONNES OF FOOD WASTE

Australia creates about **7.6 million tonnes** of food waste each year. That's more than **300 kilograms** per person!

7.6
million tonnes

9

Bad for the Environment

Dumping that uneaten piece of fruit in the ground, either into a compost heap at home or in landfill, might seem like a good idea. But when it decomposes, the rotting food creates methane gas. This is a **greenhouse gas** that contributes heavily to **climate change**.

As an apple rots, it creates small amounts of methane gas.

A large pile of food creates a larger amount of methane gas as it rots.

More greenhouse gases are made by food loss and food waste than by flying planes or by producing plastic products. Stopping food loss and food waste would have the same effect as taking one-quarter of all the cars off roads around the world.

HOW LANDFILL AFFECTS CLIMATE CHANGE

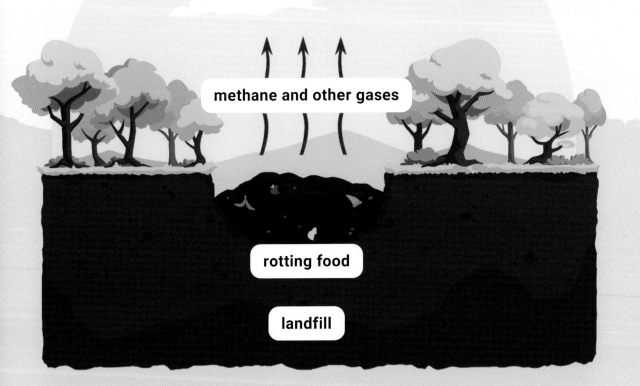

atmosphere

methane and other gases

rotting food

landfill

Rotting food in landfill creates methane and other gases, which rise into the atmosphere and contribute to climate change.

A Waste of Money

When you throw food away, you're also throwing away money. And not just the amount of money you or your family spent on the food, but the amount of money needed to produce, transport and store the food.

Farmers often need to buy expensive machinery to produce and transport food. They also need to buy feed for their animals, pay for fuel for their vehicles, and pay workers to help them on the farm. A lot of this money is wasted if the food they grow is thrown away.

Expensive machinery is often needed so farmers can produce our food.

Today, each Australian family throws away an average of $2500 worth of food in a year. In Aotearoa New Zealand, each family wastes about $1500 worth of food in a year. Imagine what your family could spend that money on instead.

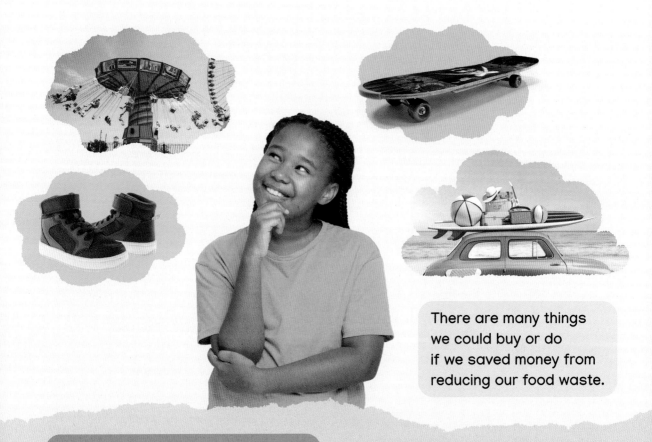

There are many things we could buy or do if we saved money from reducing our food waste.

THE COST OF FOOD WASTE

It has been estimated that food waste costs Australia around **$36 billion** each year. That amount of money could build about **36 new hospitals** each year.

$36 billion = 36 hospitals

Causes of Food Loss and Food Waste

Farming

Farming can cause food loss in several ways. Some farmers throw away food that doesn't look perfect – for example, cucumbers with unusual curves or apples that are very small. They do this because they think supermarkets won't buy this food to sell to their customers.

Some farmers don't have storage spaces to keep food fresh in extreme heat or cold. In these conditions, the food can rot or be ruined.

Sometimes, food loss happens for reasons farmers can't control. Floods, droughts and other natural disasters, or swarms of **pests**, such as mice or grasshoppers, can ruin crops so they have to be thrown away.

A farmer examines damaged corn plants after unexpected early snow.

The Way Food Is Sold

The way food is sold can also cause waste. Sometimes, supermarkets throw away fruit and vegetables that don't look perfect because they think customers won't buy them. Dairy products or meat are sometimes discarded because they are nearing their **use-by dates**, even though the food is still safe to eat.

Foods that are not perfect are known as "uglies".

Some restaurants and hotels serve large meals or "all you can eat" **buffets** to attract customers, who think they are getting a good deal. But they can't always eat everything on their plates, so the food is wasted.

Foods are still good right up until their use-by dates.

Buffets can be a source of food waste when people don't finish all the food they chose.

A Throwaway Society

Today, we live in a "throwaway society". We throw away our electronic devices because we want the latest ones. We throw away torn clothing instead of getting it mended.

We do the same with food. Some people buy and cook too much food, even when they know some will be thrown away. They might buy food they don't want or need, just because they've seen it on TV or social media, or they're tempted by special offers at the supermarket.

Sometimes, people don't store or cook fresh food properly after they've bought it. This is known as "food **spoilage**". Spoilt food can't be eaten and must be thrown away.

Many of us throw away uneaten food from our dinner plates or in our lunch boxes, without thinking about the problems it causes.

It's easy to be tempted by special offers at the supermarket.

Governments

Local governments are responsible for collecting the waste from our homes. However, some councils may not provide separate bins for food waste, so this waste gets put in with the other rubbish. Even if councils do provide bins for food waste, people may need more information about what can and can't be put in these bins.

When food isn't put in the right bin, it ends up in landfill.

Food that goes into the wrong bin ends up in landfill.

CHOOSING THE RIGHT BIN

Most local councils around Australia provide households with three different bins to put their waste in: one for waste that can be **recycled**; one for green waste such as **compost**; and one for waste that can only go into **landfill**. In some countries, such as Sweden, households have five bins just for recycling, with separate bins for paper, plastic, metals, clear glass and coloured glass.

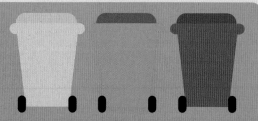

How to Fix Food Loss and Food Waste

The same people and groups that cause food loss and food waste can also help to fix the problems.

Farmers can make sure the food they produce is stored in places where extreme cold and heat won't cause spoilage.

Farmers can do two things with fruit and vegetables that don't look perfect enough to sell to shops and supermarkets. They could donate the food to **charities,** or sell it at farmers' markets. People who go to farmers' markets like to directly support farmers, and they are often less fussy about only wanting to buy "perfect" looking food.

Farmers can sell their "ugly" fruit and vegetables at farmers' markets.

Supermarkets could sell food that's nearing its use-by date at cheaper prices to encourage people to buy it, instead of letting it go to waste.

They can sell "uglies" – fruit or vegetables that don't look perfect – at cheaper prices, too.

Restaurants could serve smaller meals. And shops, supermarkets and restaurants could all donate leftover food to charities that give the food to people who can't afford to buy it.

Supermarkets can sell fruit and vegetables that are less fresh at a cheaper price.

"Uglies" can be sold at cheaper prices because they don't look perfect.

SELLING "UGLY" FRUIT

Supermarkets and other organisations have done a lot of research into how to sell "ugly" fruit. They've found that if shoppers see imperfect fruit and vegetables among better–looking ones, they will always choose the better ones. But if "ugly" fruits are separated and labelled as "ugly", shoppers will buy them to save money.

To stop wasting food, we can all choose to shop more carefully and more often, so food doesn't spoil before we use it.

Thinking about what we need to buy and making a shopping list would help. Not shopping for food when you're hungry would help, too.

When we use a shopping list we can shop more carefully.

When preparing food at home, we can make smaller meals. And we can save leftovers to eat later, rather than throwing uneaten food away.

If fresh food is about to spoil, we could make it into a vegetable soup or a fruit smoothie.

Making a meal with fresh food that's about to spoil is a good way to reduce waste.

Food waste and food loss won't be solved without the help of governments. Local councils should educate people about how to dispose of their food waste properly.

Using different bins to dispose of waste helps to reduce the amount that goes to landfill.

Instead of dumping the waste in landfill, councils could compost it correctly, and reduce the methane gas it creates.

Today, around one billion people around the world don't have enough food to eat. You might think that's because not enough food is produced, but there's more than enough food to feed everyone. Governments can work together to take food from where it's wasted to where it's needed.

Hungry people line up for donated food in the Democratic Republic of Congo.

Who Is Fixing the Problems Now?

OzHarvest

OzHarvest is a charity that was started in 2004 by Ronni Kahn. Ronni had an **event planning** business in Sydney, Australia, and she noticed a lot of food was thrown out at the end of her events. She knew that other food businesses must be wasting food, too. So she started driving around Sydney in a van, picking up leftover food from events and giving it to charities that helped people in need.

Ronni Kahn

OzHarvest helps to reduce the amount of food wasted by passing it on to people who need it.

Today, OzHarvest has many volunteers who collect food from supermarkets, cafes, delis, restaurants, airlines, hotels and other food businesses in cities around Australia.

OzHarvest volunteers collect food from all around Australia.

OzHarvest also runs education programs in schools and communities to show people how to stop wasting food.

FEAST

OzHarvest runs a free educational program for schools called FEAST. Students can learn more about food waste and healthy food, and also cook with their friends!

Goterra

In 2014, Olympia Yarger started Goterra, a food technology business, in Canberra, Australia. Goterra uses insects to try to fix the problem of food waste.

Growing up, Olympia wanted to be a sheep farmer, and she went to university to study farming. She soon realised that feeding farm animals was very expensive. She couldn't afford to have a sheep farm.

Olympia Yarger

Olympia was also very concerned about climate change. So, she combined her two passions. Olympia started a fly farm, where she fed food waste to flies! It was cheaper than raising sheep, but it was still a type of farming.

Fly farming is one way to reduce food waste.

Olympia discovered that the flies that ate food waste became very **rich** in **protein** and were a good type of food for large farm animals, such as cattle and sheep. Also, the waste the flies created could be used as **fertiliser** to help crops grow.

Olympia's company then developed technology to allow farmers to use food waste to make fertiliser on their farms.

Using food waste in this way helps to reduce the amount of greenhouse gases that go into the atmosphere.

These fly **pupae** are nearly ready to become adult flies at the Goterra fly farm.

BUGS FOR BREAKFAST!

One day, you may happily eat a bowl of insects for breakfast! Insects such as bugs contain a lot of protein and are eaten in many places in Asia and Africa. If Western countries want more sustainable farming, then insect farms may be the way to go.

What Can You Do?

The problems of food loss and food waste may be very big, but you can still do your bit to help.

Email Your Local Council

You could send an email to your local council, like this one, about the need for more compost bins.

Dear Councillors,

I think our council should give every household a compost bin, so that people can get rid of wasted food in a way that's useful.

People could put their kitchen scraps and other leftover food in the compost bin. When the food has been composted, they could put the compost on the soil in their gardens to help grow plants.

For people who live in apartments, a big compost bin could be put outside the apartment block for everyone who lives there. The compost could be put on the gardens around the apartments.

Kind regards,
Emily

Make Changes at School

You and your classmates can do things at school to reduce food waste. You could do a class food audit. An audit is an inspection of, or a close look at, something.

How to Do a Class Food Audit

Goals

1 To measure how much food you and your classmates waste in a week

2 To reduce the amount of food wasted

You Will Need

- uneaten food from you and your classmates' lunch boxes

- a device with a camera

- pen and paper

1   Tell everyone in your class to bring their lunches to school every day for a week. (Ask your teacher for help with this step.)

2   At the end of lunchtime on Monday, ask everyone to take a photo of any uneaten or half-eaten food left in their lunch boxes before they throw it into the compost bin. Repeat this step each day for the rest of the week.

3   At the end of the week, have everyone look at their five photos and write down all the food they didn't eat that week (don't include apple cores, banana peels or food wrapping).

Wasted Food –
Monday 15th to Friday 19th
   1 banana
   6 crackers
   half a salad roll
   1 tub of yogurt
   12 carrot sticks

4   As a class, make a list of the types of food that were wasted. Is there a most common food that is wasted? Discuss why you and your classmates left food uneaten. Was it because you were full? Are you leaving the same types of food uneaten every day because you don't like them?

5   For the next week, ask your classmates to try to pack only as much food in their lunch boxes as they know they will eat, and not to bring foods they know won't get eaten.

6   Repeat steps 2 and 3.

7   At the end of the second week, ask everyone how much food they wasted compared to the first week. Discuss the results as a class. Did you and your classmates find you wasted less food in the second week? Why?

How Change Happens

Food loss and food waste are big problems. So much money and so many resources are wasted when food is thrown away. Decomposing food waste is bad for the environment. Many people don't have enough food, while others have so much it's thrown away. But like most problems, there are solutions.

Everyone can do their part to reduce food waste in their own homes. People can also ask their governments to create new laws to reduce food waste. And they can ask their local supermarket managers what they are doing to reduce waste. That's how change happens.

Individuals, governments and supermarkets all need to play their part in reducing food waste.

Glossary

buffets (*noun*) — large tables of food that people can serve themselves from

charities (*noun*) — organisations that help people in need

climate change (*noun*) — changes in Earth's weather patterns

compost (*noun*) — a mixture of broken-down plants and food scraps

event planning (*noun*) — the job of organising parties and other gatherings of many people

fertiliser (*noun*) — a substance that is added to soil to help plants grow

greenhouse gas (*noun*) — a gas that traps heat in Earth's atmosphere

landfill (*noun*) — an area of land where a large amount of rubbish is buried under the ground

pests (*noun*) — insects or animals that destroy crops

protein (*noun*) — a substance animals and humans need to help them grow and stay healthy

pupae (*noun*) — young insects living in hard cases or cocoons while they prepare to change into their adult forms

resources (*noun*) — supplies of things that are useful, such as water or electricity

rich (*adjective*) — full of healthy substances

scarce (*adjective*) — not common; hard to find

spoilage (*noun*) — when food goes bad or rotten and it can no longer be used

use-by dates (*noun*) — the dates when products stop being fresh enough to safely use

Index